FIRST FACTS
CASTLES

Written by Chris Madsen
Illustrated by Brian Hoskins

© 1992 Henderson Publishing Limited

Woodbridge, England *Publishing*

THE FAMILY

William and his sister Joan live in a huge stone castle. But they don't have it all to themselves, even though it belongs to their family. It's more like a village than a big private house. Their parents, and some uncles and aunts and cousins, live right at the heart of the castle, but all the other people in the village have a place somewhere in the castle, too.

It's surprising how many people there are - not forgetting the animals! There are horses for riding, chickens for eggs, cows for milk, pigs for meat, and even sheep for wool. This means there must be grooms and milkmaids, swineherds and shepherds too.

The castle village needs carpenters and cooks, butchers and bakers and candle-makers. And then there are the soldiers. Everybody has a job to do. Together, they work to keep the whole community healthy and safe from enemies. Can you think what other jobs have to be done?

What do William and Joan do, all day long? They don't go to school, because there isn't a proper school. While they are young, they can run around anywhere they want, helping or watching other people at work. One day, they may have a castle of their own - perhaps even this one - so they need to learn as much as they can about what everybody does.

In this book, you will find out about castle life, too.

...stle is a safe place surrounded by wild forest and countryside. Some of the land round about is ploughed to grow grain and other crops. There are all kinds of dangers out there, - wild animals like wolves and bears, and wild people like brigands and bandits. Sometimes a greedy neighbour sends an army to try to capture the castle and its lands.

During the day, some of the animals are taken out to graze, and people go out hunting for meat and fruit and herbs, and to gather wood for the fires.

Visitors come and go. Traders may come with salt or spices for the kitchen, or rich material for new dresses. They'll be tired after walking or riding for many days, and will be given food and somewhere to sleep for a night or two.

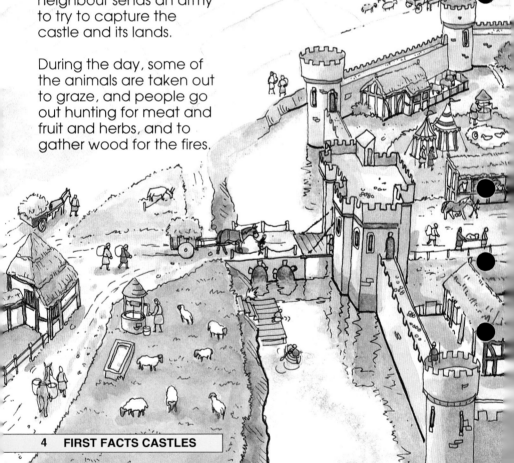

When night falls, the people who belong here - like William and Joan - are tucked up safely inside the high walls and the moat. The gates are shut and barred, and guards are posted to watch for danger.

Some people live outside the walls. Those who grow corn for the castle village, and the foresters, charcoal-burners and shepherds, may work too far away to return each evening, so they have small cottages and huts in the woods and fields. If there is a special danger, like a battle with a neighbour, they come to stay inside the high walls until it's safe to go home.

THE MOAT

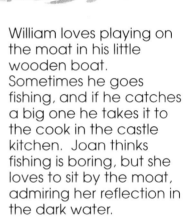

The castle where William and Joan live has a wide, deep **moat** around the outside. There is just one bridge across it, leading to the big gate.

But the stone bridge doesn't go all the way across. Part of it is made of wood, attached to strong chains. Each night this wooden part, called the **drawbridge**, is pulled up by the chains so nobody can cross the moat. It fits over the gate to make it even more difficult for unwelcome guests to get in.

The moat helps to keep people out, and its water is used for washing. Everybody enjoys eating the fish that live in the moat, too. It isn't nice clean water that we'd like to drink, because all the waste from the castle goes into it, too! So where does the castle's drinking-water come from?

William loves playing on the moat in his little wooden boat. Sometimes he goes fishing, and if he catches a big one he takes it to the cook in the castle kitchen. Joan thinks fishing is boring, but she loves to sit by the moat, admiring her reflection in the dark water.

Today, she's hoping to spot the comb she lost last week. Lots of things get lost in the moat. They may stay there for hundreds of years, until the moat dries up and people far in the future find them.

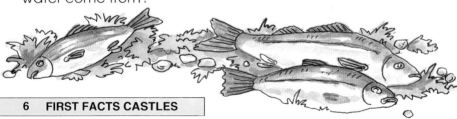

When the castle is under attack, the moat prevents enemies from getting close enough to the walls to climb up. It's not easy to swim, with heavy iron armour on! It also means that they can't bring a battering-ram near enough to break through the wall.

THE OUTER WALL

The outer wall goes right around the castle-village. There's a big gatehouse in front, where everybody who goes in and out must walk or ride past the guards on duty. As well as thick oak doors, there's an iron shutter called the **portcullis**, which can be dropped very quickly to prevent people getting in - or escaping!

Strangers who come to the gate must speak to the guards, who decide whether to let them in or not. The guards know most people who come, because they have visited before or because they live there.

Some parts of the wall are double, like a long house, with a path on top of the roof. In Summer, these paths are a lovely place to walk. William often climbs up one of the dark towers and comes out in bright sunlight on top of the wall.

Lower down, there are tall slits in the wall, just wide enough to poke an arrow through. When there's trouble, the bowmen shoot arrows through the holes at enemies outside. Why do you think the holes are made this shape, rather than round or square?

The outer wall is the first part of the castle to be damaged in an attack, so it has to be as strong as can be. When the water in the moat is low, men go out to mend the bottom of the wall.

The towers are arranged so that no part of the wall is out of sight. They give a view of the land round about, which is kept clear of trees so nobody can creep close unseen.

There are secret small doors in the wall, called **sally-ports**, where people can sneak out in an emergency.

THE OUTER BAILEY

The space inside the outer wall is called the **outer bailey**. This is a bustling place, full of small houses, stables and workshops. Most of the ordinary people live and work here. There is a blacksmith's and a pottery, and a bakery too.

William comes here to practise riding, under the eye of his father's best horsemen. One day soon, the sergeant at arms will begin teaching him how to use a big two-handed sword. Joan is chatting to her friend, Margaret, who has brought her mother's spinning-wheel outside to work in the fresh early-morning air. When the wool is spun, it will be woven into cloth to make a new shirt for Margaret's father, who is one of the castle guards.

While the horses are exercised, the stables are being cleaned out. The old straw is loaded onto a wooden wagon and taken out to spread on the fields. When the wagon comes back, it will bring bags of corn to add to the store that is kept in the castle **dungeons**.

Today, Joan and her brother can see that a big crowd has gathered around a man who came through the gate when it was opened at sunrise. He visits the castle every year, selling charms and medicines. First, he will swap some of his stock in return for having his shoes mended, and perhaps get a bread-and-cheese breakfast in the outer bailey. Then he hopes to sell something to the castle owners. Tomorrow, he will set out to ride his donkey to the next castle many miles away. When he has nothing left to sell, he goes home to a town by the sea, where he buys more goods from sailors.

THE INNER BAILEY

The grown-ups in William and Joan's family mostly stay inside the **inner bailey**, kept apart from the bustling outer bailey by another high wall. Here, the family and their special guards and servants live more quietly, away from the noisy crowds outside. The ladies stroll and chat, or perhaps sit in the sun to do their sewing when the weather is fine.

Young men enjoy sports such as falconry. There are strict rules about owning hawks. An Earl can have a peregrine; a Lady has a merlin; a priest has a sparrow-hawk; and almost anybody can hunt with a kestrel. When William learns falconry, he'll begin with a hobby. Only the King is allowed to hunt with an eagle.

William and Joan are keeping clean in their best clothes, because some special guests are coming to stay. While they wait, they're playing with a piece of string. This is a cat's cradle. Other children are playing games, too. Some of them are still played today. Can you name them?

Cooing noises come from the dovecot, where pigeons are reared for special feasts, and there are buzzing beehives which give lovely sweet honey for making puddings or spreading on bread.

Honey is also used to make a strong sweet drink called mead. The castle has a **brew-house** to make beer, and there is a vineyard outside for growing grapes to make wine.

The sunny walls of this sheltered courtyard are a good place to grow special fruit, perhaps even peaches.

The tallest building of all is set like a bull's eye right in the middle. This is the **Keep**, where William and Joan's family lives. It is a high tower, with turrets and defences of its own. Inside, there are all the rooms that most of our homes have today - but only a few rich people enjoyed such great luxury when this castle was built.

There is the **Great Hall**, where banquets are held, with kitchens close by. Above the hall are the private rooms where the family lives and sleeps.

It's nearly always cold inside the thick stone walls. In winter, huge fires help to keep off the chill. In the cellars, it is even colder - almost as cold as a refrigerator - so beer and some kinds of food can be stored there for many months.

There's a private chapel for the family, with its own priest, and the keep has its very own water supply from a well that goes in the ground below.

The keep is very strong. Soldiers can march around the flat roof, safe behind the battlements, and there are slits in the tower walls where archers can fire arrows through. The long flight of stone steps, where Joan is sitting, has a little drawbridge at the top just in front of the door.

What makes this castle keep so strong? It was built first of all, before the two walls and the moat were added. Castles like this grew very slowly. There were no bulldozers or cranes, and it might take hundreds of years to finish the building work.

THE GREAT HALL

There's a banquet in the **Great Hall** tonight. The fires are blazing, and smoky torches are burning brightly in the iron rings on the walls. Everybody wears their best clothes, and the special plates have been brought out. Joan and William are there, too, joining in the feast.

Sweating servants hurry everywhere, carrying food on wood or metal plates from the kitchen to the long tables. They bring jugs of wine and beer to fill drinking-goblets and horns.

There is plenty of meat to eat. In the middle is a huge roast boar, with dozens of smaller roasted beasts and birds up and down the table. There is also a lot of bread and fruit and nuts, but there aren't many vegetables - and no potatoes at all. Can you think why?

While people eat and drink, musicians blow pipes and pluck stringed instruments. The pedlar who arrived early this morning is also a clever juggler. He's earning a good dinner - and perhaps some money, too - by juggling balls for the household and their guests.

The big dogs are having a wonderful time, chewing bones thrown to them by the lord's guests. But they aren't pets. Like everybody else, they have a job to do. The dogs were out all week helping the hunters to catch the meat for tonight's feast. The hawks helped, too, by catching small birds and rabbits.

There will be a lot of clearing-up to do tomorrow! Extra help comes from the people of the outer bailey, and a lot of them are already helping here tonight.

THE KITCHEN AND SCULLERY

The kitchen in the keep is where food is cooked for the castle. There's no running water, electricity or gas. Water must be carried from the well in wooden buckets, and all the cooking is done with wood fires.

Everybody does as much work as they can during the day, when it's light, and the kitchen workers begin lighting fires very early in the morning. After dinner, it will be too dark to see. Have you ever tried washing up in the dark?

Washing-up is a full-time job for scullions in the scullery. There's no washing-up liquid, and not much hot water. Greasy metal pots are scrubbed with water and ashes - called 'pot-ashes' - which become soapy when they mix with fat. Burnt pans are scoured with sand.

Meat is roasted on a spit in front of the fire, turned over and over by a red-faced boy. He wraps his hands in wet cloths to keep them from roasting, too! A huge iron pot hangs over the fire, for making soup or stew. There's an oven with its own fire underneath, for baking bread and pies.

Bunches of herbs hang from the walls. Sacks of flour and other dry foods are piled around the walls and in small rooms around the main kitchen. The cook checks them every week to make sure they aren't going mouldy or being nibbled by insects.

All the food has to be grown or caught. If something runs out, the cook or her mistress can't dash to the shops as we do. Everything that comes in is noted down so it can be crossed off when it's used. The clerk keeps a record, so the castle-owner always knows exactly how much food there is.

THE BED CHAMBERS

Ordinary homes are usually just one big room - even the animals may share it, and in winter they help to keep the people warm! Ordinary people think it's a funny idea to be alone.

Rich people may have a whole room for their own use. Here in the castle the lady has a **solar**, a bed-sitting room where she sleeps at night and where her servants help her during the day.

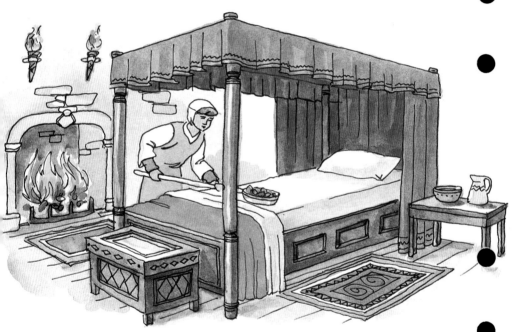

The bed, with its heavy mattress filled with straw or horsehair, is a great luxury.
This room is small enough to heat with a fire, but it's very draughty because there's no glass in the window.

In bed at night, the lady can keep out most of the draughts by closing the heavy bed-curtains around her. In winter, the bed may be warmed for her with a hot stone or a pan of coals moved over the mattress.

Another luxury is the great wooden bath, filled with warm water by a line of servants carrying buckets from the kitchen.

The two children are awaiting their turn in the bath. They'll use the same water, because it would be a waste of all that work to throw it away after just one person. Soap is made with fat and the 'pot-ashes' from the wood fires. It smells horrible. People don't have baths often, which isn't very surprising. How do they empty the bath?

The lady of the castle has another luxury - her own lavatory, called a **garde-robe**. It's just a wooden seat with a hole in it, which leads to a hole in the wall. Ordinary people have no special place for a lavatory.

LESSONS IN THE KEEP

Because William and Joan's father is a lord, they have to learn more than other children. As well as riding, hunting and fighting, William learns to read and write and do sums. Joan shares these lessons; when he's learning to lead a hunt or lead an army, she practises her sewing and singing.

It's the priest's job to teach the children their 'school' lessons, for he is one of the few people who can read and write. There are no story-books to read. Probably the only book in the castle is the big bible in the chapel, hand-written by monks in a monastery.

Parchment, made of thin layers of sheep's skin, is used for writing on, with ink made of soot or burnt bones. It's far too precious to waste on lessons, so the children practise writing their letters with a piece of chalk stone, or scratch with a stick in the dust.

They also learn about the movements of the sun and moon, planets and stars, because this is how travellers find their way.

Every little bit that the children can learn may matter one day, when they're grown up. If somebody is ill or hurt, their life could depend on Joan knowing the right herbs to use and where to find them. If William's army is going into battle, he could lose if he doesn't know how to read the clouds and tell what the weather is going to do.

Even though the castle has other people to do the work, the lord and lady should understand something about each person's job, so that they can give sensible orders.

THE ARMOURY

The armourer looks after the **armoury**, where all the weapons are kept. He's hard at work today, because of news that an enemy army is coming. He must make sure there are enough spears, swords, bows and arrows for all the men so that they can help to guard the castle or fight to defend it. The knights look after their own armour and weapons, but the armourer takes care of the rest.

Even in times of peace, the armoury is a busy place. The air rings with the sound of the hammer, beating iron plates of armour or helmets into shape. Swords must be kept sharp and free of rust so that they can be ready to use the moment they are needed. There can never be enough arrows, and the bows and their strings have to be kept supple and strong. Leather and metal shields need constant care, too.

Then there's leather and metal to be cleaned in the stables. The horses' harness, saddles and other tack are polished and oiled every day to keep them strong.

The horses didn't go out today, though. They're snorting and pawing the ground, because they've caught the feeling of excitement in the castle.

Each morning, the horses are saddled up and taken out for a run. When they come back, they must be groomed, fed and watered, while the tack is cleaned.

The war-horses are big and heavy, strong enough to carry a man wearing a heavy iron suit of armour, plus his massive sword and shield. They may even have armour of their own, such as a spiked helmet and leg-guards to protect them in a battle.

THE DUNGEONS

Down in the cellars, or dungeons, the clerk is walking around with the lord, checking stores of food and other things.

Now, it's late autumn, and the harvest has been good. There are sacks of grain, bags of turnips and little sour green apples, with small sacks of nuts and hard berries, and even some strings of dried mushrooms. There are even a few small bags of dried beans and peas.

There will be plenty of bread, anyway, and there are two small barrels of precious butter in an extra-cold corner, with hard yellow cheeses stored next to them. Some of the bees' honey is stored in pottery jars.

A hunting party went out before dawn, to catch as much as possible. If there's a siege, they won't be able to hunt again until it's over. Space has been made for hanging carcasses of deer, wild pigs or birds, or anything else they bring home.

William's out in his boat, fishing, and Joan is helping to find acorns for the pigs.

If the castle runs out of wild meat, there are pigeons in the dovecot and chickens, small pigs and other animals in the bailey. Live animals have to be fed, though. Pigs and chickens can eat stale food, or scraps that nobody wants. The milk-cow, and the sheep, can have some of the horses' hay - as long as there's enough left in the great stack in the outer bailey.

Other stores are just as important, such as wood for cooking - and for working the fires in the smithy and the armoury, so that the weapons can be mended! What else can you think of?

THE SIEGE

Beyond the castle walls, the enemy army has set up camp and is getting ready to attack.

Everybody got safely inside, and the Outer Bailey is very crowded with all the extra people and animals.
The enemy will steal anything left outside, so the people have sensibly destroyed what they can't bring with them so that it cannot help the enemy.

All the men must now fight to defend their castle. This is what the armourer is ready for. He's given out weapons and armour to the army, and now hands out the rest to some farmers who have just arrived.

William is too young to fight, but his job is to make sure the bowmen have enough arrows. His sister will be safe inside the Keep with the other noblewomen.

Every battlement of the outer wall bristles with bows and spears. Lower down, archers man the loopholes. From the bulging outer walls of the towers, men can watch the moat and every inch of the wall.

Men inside the wall can't see what's happening near to the wall on the other side.

The drawbridge of the **gatehouse** is up, and the gatehouse is full of soldiers. But there are some special tricks here. On the roof, a great wooden catapult is wound up ready to hurl huge stones onto anyone below.

There's a great iron cauldron of fat and oil, with a fire underneath to heat it up. If the enemies do manage to break through the gate, boiling oil can be poured onto them through a trap door above their heads - a horrible death! There are holes here too, called **murder holes**, where arrows can be fired down.

THE BATTLE

The enemy is well-equipped with machines for attacking a castle.

They've built a huge cross-bow. It shoots a bolt carrying burning cloth high over the wall to try to set fire to wooden buildings inside.

Catapults can hurl stones hard against the wall, to make holes for men to rush through. The monster catapult, called a trebuchet, throws big boulders over the wall to crash inside the bailey.

Some enemy soldiers are pushing a tall tower on wheels - called a **belfry** - into the moat. If they can get it against the wall, they could swarm right over the wall.

While they're getting ready, their archers keep shooting from behind wooden shields. They want the defenders to keep their heads down until it's too late.

Fire is a powerful weapon for both sides. How do you stop a fire?

While the attackers try to burn the castle, the defenders have managed to burn their belfry. Somebody sneaked out of a sally-port in the dark, and built a fire under it. Who was it? Now a hail of arrows stops the enemy soldiers getting water from the moat to put out the flames.

The attackers have nearly broken the drawbridge chain, so they all go to attack the gatehouse. Now the defenders have to use all the tricks and booby-traps here.

If the enemy manages to get into the outer bailey, the people will squeeze inside the second, higher wall.

PEACE AGAIN

The enemy has given up and gone away, and the castle-village is cleaned and tidied. Farmers have gone back to their cottages outside the walls, and the strongest men are finishing off the repair work. The blacksmith is making a new and stronger chain for the drawbridge.

The lord is walking on the **battlements** with his sergeant, talking about some ideas he got from the short siege. William's sharp eyes had spotted a new and strange kind of iron catapult that fired iron balls. Did you see it? His father believes the wall should be made thicker. The sergeant has some ideas, too; he'd like the drawbridge chain to have a shield.

It looks as if the castle defences might be changed slightly. But everyday life will continue much as before, ruled by crops and the seasons, and the speed at which a person and an animal can work or walk.